FAITH, FLAWS & FLOWS

ECHOES OF A CHRISTIAN POET

DáSean Lindell Clark

This book is a work of poetry reflecting personal faith, experiences, and creative expression. While rooted in lived moments, some details have been shaped for artistic purposes.

Scripture quotations, if any, are from the Holy Bible, the New Living Translation® (NLT®), New International Version (NIV®), King James Version® (KJV®), New King James Version® (NKJV®), English Standard Version® (ESV®), and Tree of Life Version® (TLV®).

Published by Daseanimation LLC
United States of America

First Edition, 2026

Foreward

5 years ago the Lord told me that my future husband would honor Him through self-control and would love my natural hair. I had forgotten that promise— until I saw it fulfilled in DáSean. In September of 2023, my husband and I matched on two different Christian dating apps, both seeking a Jesus-centered relationship. From our first date, there was not only an undeniable spark, but a deep sense of peace. Although we both carried baggage from our pasts, I was met with patience, consistency, and intentional love. 8 months into our courtship we got married! God's faithfulness shaped not only our relationship, but also the man behind these pages.

Faith, Flaws, and Flows is a reflection of DáSean's continued sanctification in Christ. The first section, *Faith,* is a collection of reverent praise for the Lord as our faithful Savior. The next section, *Flaws,* particularly weighed on my heart; it holds poems of lament— expressions of inner collapse and sin which reminded me of moments in my life where I felt unworthy of God's presence. These pages do not shy away from grief. *Flows,* on the other hand, offers a lighter tone— raps, culture, and fun— honest expressions of freedom found in Christ.

Watching DáSean labor over this book has been a testimony in and of itself. He worked day and night—writing between his daily responsibilities, revising relentlessly, and seeking Jesus through it all.

I pray that readers find themselves somewhere within these pages— in praise, in lament, and in the flow of joy that only the Holy Spirit can give. We will never be perfect, but as we pick up our cross daily and begin again, we'll find strength in the Lord– our perfect peace.

~ Amber D. Clark, the Author's Wife

CONTENTS

Echoes (noun): *the sounds that remain after the original source is gone— repetitions that carry meaning, memory, and truth beyond the initial event...*

<u>Beginnings</u>

Thank you for taking the time to read my labor of love, let alone this brief intro to it. For years I've desired to write and illustrate my own book. As I set out to make this dream a reality, it dawned on me I was writing something more than just a collection of poems– these were my ***echoes***: ~150 pages of lived **Faith** under fire, **Flaws** exposed, and **Flows** from the rhythm of life's ups & downs.

Many of these poems were written in real time– mid-mistake, mid-prayer, and mid-reflection. They emerged from my walk– imperfect but progressing; however these reflections aren't mine alone. They mirror the same exact conflicts and breakthroughs we all face as we walk with God.

If you're anything like me, these poems are meant to sound familiar...

~ DáSean L. Clark, the Author

I

FAITH

Behold the Lamb of God, who takes away the sins of the world.

~ John 1:29

I am the door. If anyone comes through Me, he will be saved.

He will come and go and find pasture. ~ John 10:9

He Is

Yes! He is the LAMB.
He died for us; rose again.
Blessed! He is the GOAT.

Adoored

I adore you Lord.
You're the door we all come through
for life ever more.

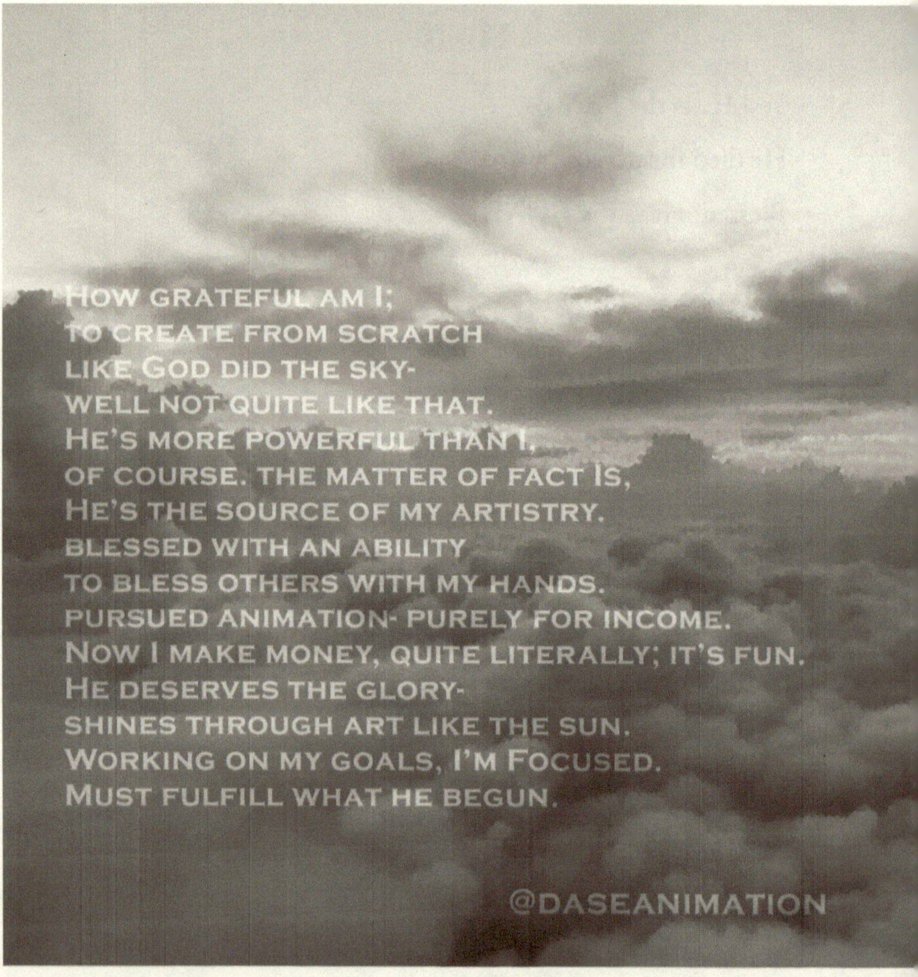

HOW GRATEFUL AM I;
TO CREATE FROM SCRATCH
LIKE GOD DID THE SKY-
WELL NOT QUITE LIKE THAT.
HE'S MORE POWERFUL THAN I,
OF COURSE. THE MATTER OF FACT IS,
HE'S THE SOURCE OF MY ARTISTRY.
BLESSED WITH AN ABILITY
TO BLESS OTHERS WITH MY HANDS.
PURSUED ANIMATION- PURELY FOR INCOME.
NOW I MAKE MONEY, QUITE LITERALLY; IT'S FUN.
HE DESERVES THE GLORY-
SHINES THROUGH ART LIKE THE SUN.
WORKING ON MY GOALS, I'M FOCUSED.
MUST FULFILL WHAT HE BEGUN.
@DASEANIMATION

How Grate

How grateful am I?
To create from scratch,
like God did the sky–
Well not quite like that,
He's more powerful than I, of course.
The matter of fact is,
He's the source of my artistry.
Blessed with an ability
to bless others with my hands.
Pursued animation– purely for income.
Now I make money, literally, it's fun.
He deserves the glory.
Shines through my art like the sun.
Working on my goals, I'm focused.
Must fulfill what He begun.

...Be strong and courageous. Do not be afraid or dismayed for the LORD your God will be with you wherever you go.

~ Joshua 1:9

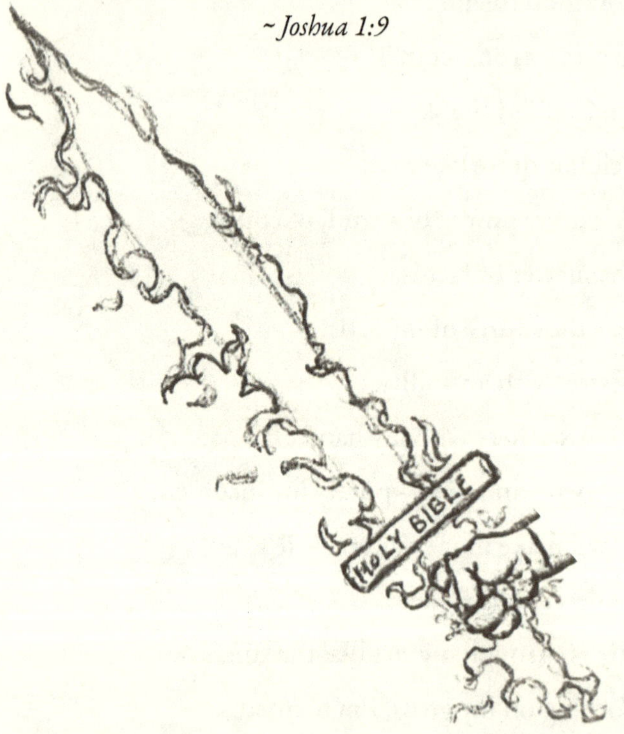

Therefore take up the full armour of God... and the sword of the Spirit, which is the Word of God. ~ Ephesians 6:13, 17

Brave and the Bold

Black by birth.
Dark as the Knight.
I was nurtured as a Christian,
To shirk & Bale from a fight.
But only when I read for myself,
with a heart contrite,
did I learn how to strike
every bat outta hell.
To take hold the sword of the spirit,
To be Brave.
To be Bold.
To be a light in shadow.
To share my faith
so you can hear it.
And declare, "*No*–
it's not who I am underneath,
but, what I do,
that defines me".

"You are the God who sees me." ~ Genesis 16:13

She [wisdom] is more precious than rubies; nothing you desire can compare to her. ~ Proverbs 3:15

He Sees

God sees me, El Roi.
Like preborn John the Baptist,
I'm jumping for joy.

3:15

Fame and stock shares,
Cant compare to wisdom gained through
"Self-care" [Read Scripture].

...new wine must be poured into new wineskins. ~ Luke 5:38

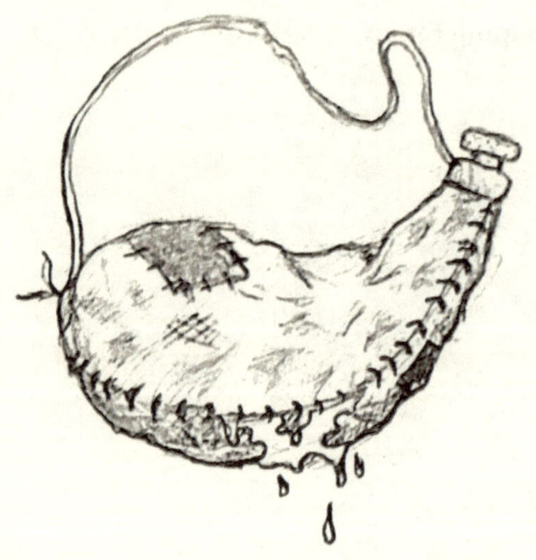

...that Christ died for our sins according to the Scriptures, and that He was buried, and that He rose again the third day according to the Scriptures. ~ 1st Corinthians 15:3-4

~~Hercules~~ Jesus Saves

We've all sinned; in need of a savior
and Jesus was it, not Hercules & his 12 labors.
Works righteousness, idolatry-- all filthy rags.
His death on a tree paid the cost.
For this, we are all glad.
'Cause 3 days later He then rose
and on the day of Pentecost,
the Spirit filled God's people;
those He chose.
Now living in our hearts,
we are God's steeple;
His humble abode.

Jesus said to them, "I am the bread of life; whoever comes to me shall not hunger, and whoever believes in me shall never thirst.
~ John 6:35

But the Helper, the Holy Spirit, whom the Father will send in my name, he will teach you all things and bring to your remembrance all that I have said to you. ~ John 14:26

Submit to the Savior

I had a sneaking suspicion that:
"Serving solves sadness."
It's the sole solution to seclusion,
'snot simply speculation.
So if you're seeking a cessation of soul-sucking sensations,
such as shame, sickness, solipsism,
solitary situations or similar synonyms,
then, at the risk of sounding silly,
Submit yourself to the Savior.
The second we accept the Holy Spirit sent to support us,
He'll sire a desire to share space with someone we trust.
We shan't succumb to seeds of suffering, suicide or lust.
Instead we secure success by
investing and sowing in
the One who sustains sanity,
and satiates our soul.
When we divest from lies sold,
we stop settling for less,
steer clear of stress,
and stand bold with strength–
Following His footsteps.

Fathers can give their sons an inheritance of houses & wealth, but only the LORD can give an understanding wife.

~ Proverbs 19:14

He who finds a wife, finds a good thing and obtains favor from the LORD. ~ Proverbs 18:22

Flesh of my Flesh

Scripture says only God can give
an understanding wife;
and if he finds one–
Outstanding! They've won at life.

Well, as I breathe and live,
I won't grieve, or diss,
or affront this Proverb.
'Cause for 8 months I courted her
'til we reached the altar.

Then rain poured from the sky,
as Heaven tore wide.
With hair oil in my eyes,
I was prone to be blind.
But this bone of my bone
lended a hand, sublime–
God's grace fore-shown to me at the time.

So yes, she's a Treasure.
He blessed us both,
impressed, beyond measure.
The love story He wrote.

Flee sexual immorality. Every other sin that a man commits is outside the body, but he who commits sexual immorality sins against his own body. ~ 1st Corinthians 6:18

For this is the will of God- your sanctification: that you should abstain from fornication. ~ 1st Thessalonians 4:3

GP+GR

With Great Power comes
Great Responsibility–
sexuality *

Abstain

Practice abstinence,
Can't get pregnant without sex.
This is common sense.

...The very hairs on your head are numbered. Don't be afraid; you are worth more than many sparrows. ~ Luke 12:7

There are six things the LORD hates, seven that are detestable to Him:... Hands that shed innocent blood. ~ Proverbs 6:16-17

Life is Valuable

Made in His Image.

Cherished from the beginning.

A Life worth Living.

Detestable

Proverbs Six:Sixteen.

Hands that shed innocent blood,

are hated by Him.

Wisdom is the principle thing; therefore acquire wisdom. And in all your getting, get understanding. ~ Proverbs 4:7

Faith and Politics

Always buried in spirituals;
Psalms and hymns my lyrical
background. It's criminal
how I finally started watching the news–
wont political before then–
but 'round 18, I was glued
to the TV screen (to CNN).
2015 I'm surprised
when Trump becomes 45.
But, I digress–
(He's not the point at this time,
and regardless of how you feel
about the Presidential seal,
Christ is still King, right?
No matter who in the Oval office
reigns supreme-like.)
So, back to this rhyme:
Leading up to voting day,
I had an open mind;
stayed open to change–
like the climate.

I wanted to be well informed
before I cast my ballot, and
question what I came to know.
So I dug into every issue
to unearth the real truth.
Into things like Gun Control,
not long after Dylann Roof;
scoped out both views of the Constitute,
to know where I land on 2A.
Then read up on Social Justice,
and police brutality
like Sandra Bland.
Did Black lives matter,
or Blue lives matter?
And what about the babies?
That's when the Prolife-bug bit me like rabies.
I investigated the claims of Prochoice groups.
Examining the slogans I'd hear them shoot.
Like "Reproductive healthcare",
"A woman's right to choose",
or "just a clump of cells"–
assertions they can't prove.
The science was clear,

and, if that wasn't enough,
the Bible *was* too!
My perspective grew
watching theological debates;
broadening my worldview
of the political landscape.
Apologetics was far from
hollow rhetoric.
I learned to defend the faith.
And with all this new wisdom,
for my ignorance, I fear, I had to repent of lies.
For I ignored sense– the preborn *human* lives.
Just like I would've been denied
way back when they'd buy and sell black skin.
We dehumanize our difference,
then justify the consequence.
We're trapped, inclined to be ensnared by sin.
"The truth will set you free."
No longer a given
to trust what others say or do.
Be it the news, or word of mouth,
you gain more if you avoid the ruse.
Benefit of the doubt.

The LORD said to Moses... "I myself will set my face against that man and will cut him off from his people; for by sacrificing his children to Molek..." ~ Leviticus 20:3

For you formed my inmost being; You knit me together in my mother's womb. ~ Psalm 139:13

Abortion

This is <u>not</u> a right.

Adoption <u>is</u> an Option.

Stop child sacrifice.

Exceptions

Kids conceived from non–

consensual conception

deserve protection.

Then God spoke all these words, saying... "Thou shalt not murder." ~ Exodus 20:13

"...do not kill the innocent and righteous. For I will not justify the wicked." ~ Exodus 23:7

Number Six

"Thou shall not murder"

Abortion murders babies–

God did not stutter.

Expedience

Get off the fence, cause

We can't murder innocence

for our convenience.

@daseanimation

Had this revelation the other night,
as I prayed for strength and insight,
of how we're spiritually akin to Hoarders.
Accustomed to the filth in every corner
of our lives- attached to folks, habits,
and behaviors hindering our drive.
We know somethings off, we want to move on
but the crap is overwhelming,
It's too daunting,
So, not knowing where to begin, we give in.
We've been here too long to change.
We settle for less, grow attached to the mess,
finding an identity in what's killing us,
We get comfortable with our surroundings.
Adapt, adjust, and decorate the outside,
As to not look and smell so robust
while the inside rots and rusts.
So if we're the Hoarders, then God's the cleaners-
He comes to help, doing what we can't on our own.
Once we accept, we may not see a difference.
He starts small at first, but over time the burden's lifted.
One by one, the trash is taken out,
separating us from the things
we found comfort in; the things that
led to doubt and low confidence.
He removes the pain, and the people,
the past, sin and shame we hold onto.

But it's not against our will. God is gentle.
Like in Hoarders, He grants us discretion:
"Can I throw this out? Yes? No??"
And He pleads, "You don't need it. Let Go."
Some people submit, grateful for the assist,
they even join in removing the filth
as they see an end to the tunnel, lit-
the new found freedom in their home.
Other people stay put, not budging,
refusing to loosen the grip on their belongings.
Irony is, the things have more of a grip on them.
That's why at the end of an episode,
some leave completely freed,
while others settle for one room cleaned.
They kick up their feet, and presume they've grown.
Then there are those off screen,
who'll never seek deliverance;
too embarrassed or stubborn to reach out.
God desires for a complete 180-
a restoration of our innermost being.
To get us back to who we were before lifes' beating.
Before we accumulated all this baggage.
He wants us to let Go, and let Him have free reign in our lives,
Unimpeded by the mess in our minds.
A hoard won't be honed in by a single soul.
We need an almighty God to take control.

Hoarders

Had this revelation the other day,
as I prayed for strength and insight,
of how we're spiritually akin to Hoarders–
accustomed to the filth in every corner
of our lives; attached to folks, habits,
and behaviors hindering our drive.
We know something's off, we want to move on,
but the *crap* is overwhelming.
It's *too* daunting.
So, not knowing where to begin, we give in.
We've been here too long to change.
We settle for less, grow attached to the mess,
finding an identity in what's killing us.
We get comfortable with our surroundings.
Adapt, decorate and adjust the outside,
so as to not look and smell so robust
while the inside rots and rusts.
So if we're the Hoarders, then God's the Cleaners–
He comes to help, doing what we can't on our own.
Once we accept, we may not see the difference.
He starts small at first,

but over time the burden's lifted.
One by one, the trash is taken out,
separating us from the things
we found comfort in; the things that
led to doubt and low confidence.
He removes the pain, and the people;
the past, sin and shame we hold onto.
But it's not against our will. God is gentle.
Like in Hoarders, He grants us discretion;
"Can I throw this out? Yes? No??"
And He pleads, "You don't need it, so Let Go."
Some people submit, grateful for the assist.
They even join in, removing the filth
as they see an end to the tunnel, lit;
the new found freedom in their home.
Other people stay put, not budging,
Refusing to loosen the grip on their belongings.
Irony is, these things have more of a grip on them.
That's why at the end of an episode,
some leave completely freed,
while others settle for only one room cleaned.
They kick up their feet, and presume they've grown.
Then there are those off screen,

who'll never seek deliverance;
too embarrassed or stubborn to reach out.
God desires a complete 180–
a restoration of our innermost being.
To get us back to who we were before life's beatings.
Before we accumulated *all* this baggage.
He wants us to let go
& let Him have free reign in our lives.
Unimpeded by the mess in our minds.

A hoard won't be honed in by a single soul,
We need an Almighty God to take control.

But one thing I do: Forgetting those things which are behind and reaching forward to those things which are ahead, I press toward the goal for the prize of the high calling of God in Christ Jesus. ~ Philippians 3:13-14

K. M. F

Keep Moving Forward,
Even when it's hard
End the cycle.
Pray to the LORD.

Make wise choices.
Only then will you see, a
Vast harvest of fruitful victories.
Incline thine ear to like-minded voices, so
Negative thoughts can wither and cease.
Go above & beyond in everything done.

For our works show just how far we've
Overcome the world- by faith in God's Son.
Reality is we must rest and be still;
Walk away from strife and quarreling.
Always give thanks, for this is God's will, &
Refuse immoral things. Reach out to Jesus.
Depend on His Holy spirit to teach and lead us.

For as a man thinketh in his heart, so is he... ~ Proverbs 23:7

The LORD is my Shephard... He maketh lie down in green pastures... I will fear no evil: for thou art with me; thy rod and thy staff they comfort me. ~ Psalm 23:1-2, 4

Reflection

Sittin' pretty, vibing to GoldenR&B–
a litany of music with soothing melody.
As I write on flash cards,
Bible verses to remember,
I think back to last Fall–
or maybe it was Winter;
back when I was enthralled,
pining to be a member of a D9 frat.
Was at their beck & call.
Was told to learn their history.
I'd scrawl down fun facts,
commit them to memory–
so I could quickly recall them
if bros ever questioned me.
I'd research day and night,
way more than Bible study.
Brainwashed, in a daze;
clouded by the devil.
I was lost, in the haze,
led astray to do evil.
But I gave Him the praise;
for like a Good Shepherd,
He allowed me to graze

once He led me out to pasture.
Now the only *crook* I like,
is the one He'll raise
to comfort and nurture,
and protect me from thieves.
Now on another note,
a different tune,
I think back even further:
I'd memorize verses from my mother,
stacked and kept,
in a light blue container;
like "*Jesus wept*",
and *Psalms 119*
(verse 105 if you want to read).
It's funny the things
that always come to mind
when you sit and think
back on old times.
What we hear and read
will always define
who we grow to be.
So take the time
and *pay* attention
with sight in hind–
for Reflection's free.

...he brought them out of their distress. He stilled the storm to a whisper; the waves of the sea were hushed. ~ Psalms 107:28-29

"Come to me, all you who are weary and burdened... and you will find rest for your souls. For my yoke is easy and my burden is light." ~ Matthew 11:28-30

Comfort in the Storm

Blessed are those who mourn,
for the Holy Ghost keeps 'em warm.
He's a comfort in the storm.
When we're weary and out-worn.
If we desire peace,
JC promised true rest;
His yoke is ease.

But God demonstrates His love for us, in that while we were still sinners, Christ died for us. ~ Romans 5:8

High and Mighty

Sin is overwhelming,
ingrained desire since a youngling.
Without a doubt, no competition,
This is the hardest game I've had to play.
A path so narrow
to avoid perdition.
And sadly it hits me
how consequential this is,
only after I'm hit with consequences of sin.
I recall those days: on the high-way,
I chose roads clouded in weed smoke
as my way of copin'.
And I'd hear from Him often.
God would speak to me vividly,
about my destiny;
about His free gift to us,
His one and only Son, Lord Jesus...
Goodness gracious, the world we live in:
Sin fills everywhere we look–
every nook, cranny, and den;
the theivin', lying, crooks,
and degens.

Everywhere I turn, the opposite of You awaits me–
to turn me back towards what hates me.
Society, ideologies,
spiritual voodoo...
But what am I to do?
Can't do it on my own.
Only You.
Only You alone,
lived the perfect life,
died the servant's death
I rightly deserved.
Lord knows I'm not worth it.
When I was high, drunk and lit,
I was shown the pit:
fire and brimstone;
gnashing of teeth to atone.
But I thank you...
I know you don't condone
of my behavior, my thoughts,
my actions or inactions.
Lord knows it's hard to do what I ought to.
But I God thank you...
above all for your compassion.
For your unending pursuit.

Do not merely listen to the word, and so deceive yourselves. Do what it says. ~ James 1:22-24

Though your sins are like scarlet, they shall be as white as snow. ~ Isaiah 1:18

A Prayer for Deliverance

God, I wanna do better.

At times my actions

mismatch my intentions–

I can be fake as pleather.

Led astray by my passions,

the desires of my flesh...

"You need more self discipline,

to stay away from the mess.

Starve yourself of sin and

crave Godliness. Lest you forget

Christ's sacrifice..."

Yes! I Need You to Survive,

and Something about that Name

brings tears of shame.

For at last in a weep,

He gave me real Peace—

what I could not grasp

through exercise in the gym every week:

Anger misplaced—at punching bags—

now rain from my face consumes snot rags.

Thank You for stillness, for calm.

For turning my clenched fists
into praying palms.
This good news
of a more abundant life
will inspire you.
It is why I write:
So think before you leap,
and watch the company you keep,
before consequences ensue.
For what you sow, you shall reap.

..."O faithless generation, how long shall I be with you? How long shall I put up with you?" ~ Mark 9:19

Untitled I

The Messiah said it best,
"How do I exist with these folk?"
Too many requests.
Too many to please.
Unfortunately I regress,
ignore the yoke,
focus on my needs,
and the mess I tote.
It takes strictness–
a foreign trait
we forsake on campus;
where they promote immorality,
instead of Jesus...

Very truly I tell you, everyone who sins is a slave to sin.

~ John 8:34

They traded the truth of God for a lie and... served the creation rather than the Creator... Although they know... those who do such things deserve death- they not only continue to do these very things but also approve of those who practice them.

~Romans 1:25, 32

I Hate ~~Sin~~

I Hate it.

I hate what it's done to my life,

and the lives of those I love.

I hate how it separates us from others,

and from God up above.

I hate how society shapes Sin to seem

not *that* bad.

And/or the way we deceive ourselves to think

a little needs to be had

in order to say we've lived.

Sin is so destructive,

oftentimes corrosive;

presents itself as a fun new thing to try–

calling on the curious cats–

then 15 years pass by,

as you futilely attempt to turn back.

It's the same reason a bully won't leave be alone,

because they've been hurt at home.

And since misery loves company,

Sin is never isolated;

it's never done alone.

Viewing smut films or hitting up sneaky links.
As said once before, our actions matter,
but so is what we think...
So what do you imagine happens
to a mind on the brink–
submerged in **a sinful culture**
that takes every time and opportunity
to pick at you like a vulture?
That expresses explicitly
that "fornication isn't *that* bad",
and "if your not having it by now
then in fact that's sad".
A culture that scoffs at purity
and praises the pride of life.
Like a wolf in sheep's clothing,
it's duplicitous in molding us to hate ourselves
by hating what's good–
the lot says do what
we rather should not.
It promotes the lusts of the flesh.
We indulge our every thought,
which can't be wrong because it's natural, right?
A culture that tells us 'just say no',

then ‘just on celebrations’,
then ‘just in moderation’,
now ‘if it’s legal, it’s a go’.
A culture more convinced by popular opinion
than an absolute moral code;
as if, for no rhyme or reason, we‘re to blindly follow
all chickens that cross the road...
What do you imagine happens to a mind
submerged in that kind of culture?
Well of course it’s left to think
right is wrong,
up is down,
wisdom has an authority-complex,
and if it feels good then say less.
I hate sin because I've been through it.
After being submerged for so long,
living Right feels strange
–we unquestionably urge to do wrong.
Sin tricks us all, and makes us its slave.
Unbeknownst to many of us,
it’s through which we all tend to behave.
So desensitized to sin,
we advertise faulty ways of thinkin’.

Then we point fingers when things go awry,
rather than take a look in the mirror,
or use our voice to speak out,
and be a gadfly against the sin we tout.
Sin is the abusive partner that means so well–
would claim to never hurt you, &
would be highly recommended if you were to ask–
but inevitably leads to death in trespass.
Furthermore, unlike covid,
we can't be saved by a mask;
there's no amount of sanitizer
or clorox to cleanse
our sinful past, present
and future sins.
Sin permeates our everyday;
our politics, internet, music and more.
It's in me, in you, and the girl next door.
...But God.
He *so* loved us.
While we blatantly disregarded Him–
the Creator of all the good gifts we enjoy–
He *so* loved us.
While we flaunted our sin–

unashamed or unaware of how it may destroy–
He *so* loved us,
that He gave His one & only Son.
For *our* sake Jesus died.
Living the life we knew better to live,
and dying the death we know
in our heart of hearts
we deserve to die;
so that believing in Him,
we may have eternal life: Real Life.
Not a superficial,
happy-for-the-moment,
pleasing-my-desires,
living "my truth" kinda life.
But abundant life in the presence
of the only One who gives life in the first place.
I hate sin,
because most days I love it.
I hate sin,
because despite His mindblowing sacrifice–
and the fact that the Creator of the Cosmos
would care about each and every one of us,
so much so that He'd lower Himself to our level,

just to die on our behalf; woe–
like a calf, we kept running into the road,
just *asking* to be hit.
Sin has us saying 'so what' and settling for less,
while God hath loved us so much
He gave *His* best.
I hate sin
because it clouds our minds from the Truth:
that Jesus loves us, and like Him
we don't need sin, sin needs us.
We need Him, & all He asks is Trust.

II

FLAWS

OnceUponATimeThereLivedAKidWhoRhymed,
AlwaysDidAsHeWasToldAndNeverCrossedTheLine.
WellUntilHeGotOldWhenItAllSeemedJust
FineToBreakTheMold. YesHeHadFlaws
ButHeLivedUpright. YetLoAndBeholdCollegeLife
GrabbedAholdAndHeldOnTightLikeARodeo-
ClownBehaviorToBeHonest. LearnedHisLesson
OnceHeBecameHaunted; GhostsFrom
ThePast-MistakesMadeThatCouldntBeChanged.
LearnedTheyreBetterToBeLaidToRest
InExchangeForAPeaceOfMind,
AndNoRegrets.
@daseanimation

Fairy Tales

Once Upon A Time
There Lived A Kid Who Rhymed;
Always Did As He Was Told
And Never Crossed the Line.
Well, That Is, Until He Got Old
When It All Seemed Just Fine
To Break The Mold.
Yes, He Had Flaws
Although He Lived Upright;
Yet Lo and Behold
The College Life Grabbed Ahold,
And Held On Tight
Like A Rodeo–
Clown Behavior, To Be Honest.
Learned His Lesson
Once He Became Haunted
By Ghosts From His Past Mistakes
That Couldn't Be Changed.
Learned They're Better to Be Laid To Rest
In Exchange For A Peace Of Mind
And No Regrets.

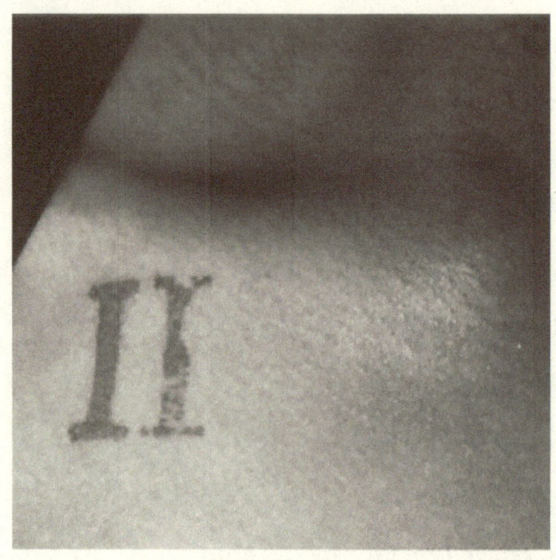

For what I want to do I do not do, but what I hate I do... For I do not do the good I want to do, but the evil I do not want to do— this I keep on doing... it is no longer I who do it, but it is sin living in me that does it. ~ Romans 7:15, 17; 19-20

II

2 is for all the times I made the wrong choice.
I chose you–
the sick, twisted desire,
the Voice in my head...
Wanted to be Good,
but did Bad instead.

Roman numeral II
One I stands perfect.
Now inked in skin–
and yes, it was worth it–
forever is a reminder of the conflict in me.
Of my blatant flaws and hypocrisy.
My tendency to be stuck between
Bad and *Better*.
Just my luck, it seems no good;
it doesn't matter,
and it never would,
whether or not I try.

FLAWS

I always give in to the ruined I:
the wrong choice– the What inside–
that I had already made up my mind to do...
Good actions I've lacked–
intentions irrelevant.
It always comes down to 2,
and guess which one I pick...

The Wrong decision,
the Wrong person.
Stuck on the same mission,
yet to learn my lesson;
oh, the games I've played...

So 2 is for all the times
I have and will face a crossroads.
It reminds me to take the road less traveled by
(I usually don't but at least I try).
While one I is in ruin,
the worst off between those,
the I that's left stands upright,
Untouched... and Unchose-
-in hindsight,
one might suppose, I... am ruined.

Be alert, be vigilant; because your adversary the devil prowls around like a roaring lion, seeking whom he may devour.

~ 1st Peter 5:8

Temptation

I strive to do right,
Stage left, the devil enters
Drags me down, hither.

The Enemy

Steal, Kill and Destroy–
Like a lion he devours;
Lyin' to ya boy.

And if your right hand causes you to stumble, cut it off and throw it away. It is better for you to lose one part of your body than for your whole body to go into hell. ~ Matthew 5:30

Right Hand

Words, words, and more words.
Writing sentences for punishment,
Hand crampin' like back in school.
I'm mad often but I cool off when
writing poems.
I won't spazz.
I don't do what you'd rather–
Like take my life,
so as to cease to bother.
A common thought that's ran
through my head– through strife,
hell and high water:
To take a knife,
and cut off the hand
that caused me to sin
again and again against others.
I can't seem to win,
though I'm finally doing better.
A cold heart gave way to cold weather
as Jesus warmed me up from inside like a sweater.
I just pray not to stray from His side,
not now, not ever.

Do not repay evil for evil or insult for insult, but give a blessing instead—it is for this reason you were called, so that you might inherit a blessing. ~ 1 Peter 3:8-9

Hurt People[2]

You bash us.
tell me I'm ugly, I'm fat,
I'm trash, plus, I'm black;
I blend in at dusk.
I'm dumb & I smile too much.
But Imma kid, I'm young
I'm just acting as such...
Just living for fun.
And now that I'm older,
I hurt ya hearts,
make your smiles smolder;
dirt from the start.
You tell me I'm heartless,
insensitive and cold,
only care 'bout myself.
But woah! Remember I was told
countlessly
how worthless I was.
So why blame me for the person you caused?
(Not you specifically,
speakin' generalities...)

The bullies bullied til the victims folded,
so we can't hate, or be mad at,
the individuals molded
by "gay" this and "fag" that..
Hurt people hurt people.
We're born ungood.
Treat others like fecal–
don't act as we should,
We must make a positive impact.
Only then can we grin,
and truly smile again...
With our hearts intact.

They are foolish, faithlesss, heartless, ruthless. ~ Romans 1:31

Every way of a man is right in his own eyes, but the LORD weighs the hearts. ~ Proverbs 21:2

[In]Sensitive

Is it what I said?
Is it what I did?
I swear my intentions
were only the best...
Fine— who cares what they think.
To heck with forgiveness.
All I need is Me, Myself,
& Most High as my witness.
Besides, what I have to say
is way more important—
Opportunities come on platters,
served in portions:
Today's a new day,
& if I mess up again
there'll always be another.
I just keep on trying;
that's how I recover.
"Hurt feelings, hearts smashed,
how do you move on?"
I say, "Oh well! Too bad.
Can't fix past wrongs.

Can't stop and dwell.
I focus on future dealings,
doing good to 'void Hell."
I'll change like the weather;
Won't Fall, that's wack.
I'll Spring to action–
And run run run
'til removed from my back
is this monkey of conviction.
Correct what I've done?
Fix the pain you've been through?
Mend broken hearts and expectations—
Uhuh, with *glue...*?
Nah, that's not on me; that on you.
My mistakes are known and my guilt is too.
But that's all I'll own;
That's all I can do.

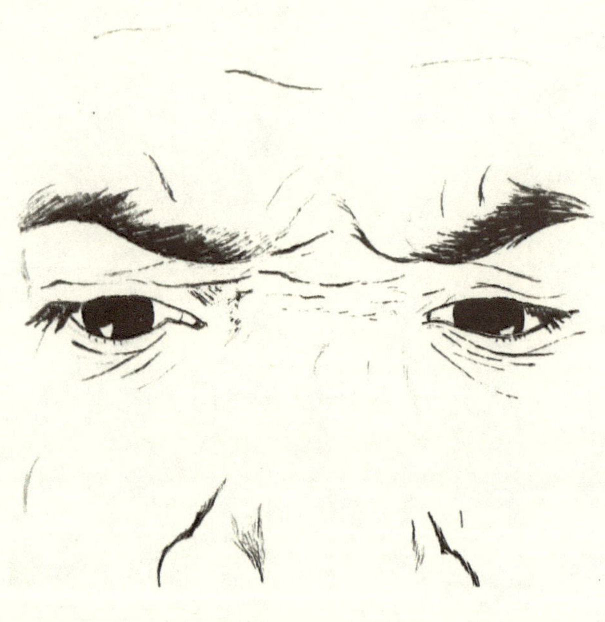

Their loyalty is divided between God and the world, and they are unstable in everything they do. ~ James 1:8

~~No~~ Rhyme or Reason

I feel fraudulent, fake
& appalled, I can't take it.
My mistakes & hypocrisy,
I know better but don't care whether
I ruin what I got going for me or not-
my witness,
and reputation,
future dreams and aspirations.
Like a rot or cancer-
I have no idea
why I do what I do;
what I know I not ought to.
An imposter with no answer.
A rhyme, no reason.

...If I go up to the heavens, you are there; if I make my bed in the depths, you are there. If I rise on the wings of the dawn, if I settle on the far side of the sea, even there your hand will guide me, your right hand will hold me fast. ~ Psalm 139:7-10

Control

Listening to Commander
by Kid Cudi.
"So in control" he sings,
mocking me,
because my life's spiraling out of it.
My soul, feeling farther from God.
I try to keep ahold,
a grip on what's right and wrong.
But behold as I live, I fight
between falling apart
and succeeding with my art...
The motivation to keep going
is found in the day to day.
Like writing my father in jail
or picking up my pay–
Checking it all off the to-do list,
and hoping for the best;
that at least by the end of day, I was conducive;
at least somewhat helpful to those around me,
and deemed not too secluded.

For the wages of sin is death... ~ Romans 6:23

So letting your sinful nature control your mind leads to death.
But letting the Spirit control your mind leads to life & peace.
~ Romans 8:6

Transgress

Wouldn't be the last day I've been enthralled
with thoughts of Hell–
I mean to say/to tell, to end it all.
Dragged off, burnt for my sins.
Would be just my luck, all things considerin'.
(Turnt up too much with so-called friends.
Gone places I should not have ever been,
with those who had bad intentions.)
Would it be a dub– a win win?
For You and me.
No more shame or guilt,
I'd finally be free.
I know You care but
I'd be outta Ya hair,
outta Ya head,
since I've messed up.
Deservin' the bed that I lay in.
The bed I made
from past transgressions.

Therefore let anyone who thinks that he stands take heed lest he fall. ~ 1st Corinthians 10:12

For if you live according to the flesh you will die; but if by the Spirit you put to death the deeds of the body, you will live.

~ Romans 8:13

Contend with Sin

I'm trash? Well don't I know it.
No surprise when I blow it-
provin' Imma disappointment.
It's a shame cause I know this
ain't a fight, that I can throw in
the towel—
wrung dry, repented.
Washed of sin;
won't contend with it.
Put to death what lies dormant—
all my deeds You deem abhorrent.

Hear me now, my children, and do not depart from the words of my mouth... lest strangers feast on your wealth and your toil enrich the house of another. ~ Proverbs 5:7, 10

For the flesh desires what is contrary to the Spirit, and the Spirit what is contrary to the flesh. They are in conflict with each other, so that you cannot do what you want.
~ Galatians 5:17

Squander

I'm mad at myself.
I keep freakin' messin' up.
Forfeitin' my wealth.

My Flesh

I wish to do better–
Don't wanna stay the same.
But my flesh don't care whether
I wish to make a change.

When wickedness comes, so does contempt, and with dishonor comes disgrace. ~ Proverbs 18:3

Adore & Abhor

Do I deserve love?
Do I deserve happiness?
I feel like Job,
save for the righteousness.
So put upon me, all of the hate
which I dished out first.
I do deserve that much,
it is my fate– no worse than death.
I've carelessly and thoughtlessly,
put no one else above me;
Lived selfishly.
Far beyond loving.

Because of the LORD's mercies we will not be consumed, for His compassions never fail. They are new every morning! Great is Your faithfulness. ~ Lamentations 3:22-23

Fire tests the purity of silver & gold, but the LORD tests the heart. ~ Proverbs 17:3

Spilled Milk

Grace poured in my cup;
Blessings wasted galore, but
God pours me back up.

By Fire

Called to do better.
To be purified by fire.
Til sin's reign retires.

Even so you also outwardly appear righteous to men, but inside you are full of hypocrisy and lawlessness.
~ Matthew 23:28

But there is another power within me that is at war with my mind. This power makes me a slave to the sin that is still within me. ~ Romans 7:23

Man vs Self

I've always related to Jykell & Hyde–
the intelligent, well-put together,
elegant doctor,
with one heck of an aside,
who led a rather undesirable
style of life...
The darkness in him,
that creepy, & grim
bleak impulse that resides
beneath the surface; that skulks behind.
Not much different than the Hulk,
Sentry, Werewolves, or SPLIT–
that alter ego the main character combats with.
I relate... heavily. Unfortunately.
There's a side of me that doesn't care
who gets hurt. It wants what it wants,
& if I'm complicit, it *will* scorch earth...
Rather, if I'm complacent,
I won't really know who's in the driver seat.
Am I faking my reality?
Biding my time, to make way for the inner me–

crosing the line at every opportunity.
To have my cake & eat it too.
Wayne by day, Bats by night.
From dusk til dawn,
I do what I like.
Like 50 by 100,
I'm divided in 2.
Half-wanting what I shouldn't.
Half-knowing it would soothe,
for a short time;
But of course, it's not prudent.
Not wise to give into.

You belong to your father, the devil... there is no truth in him. When he lies, he speaks his native language, for he is a liar and the father of lies. ~ John 8:44

...Resist the devil and he will flee from you. Draw near to God, and He will draw near to you. ~ James 4:7-8

~~Devil~~ is a Lie

Like the old serpent

lies spew from my mouth.

Mordant views I spout.

Resist

Ashamed by mistakes.

Satan's schemes, I pray away.

Thank God Jesus saves.

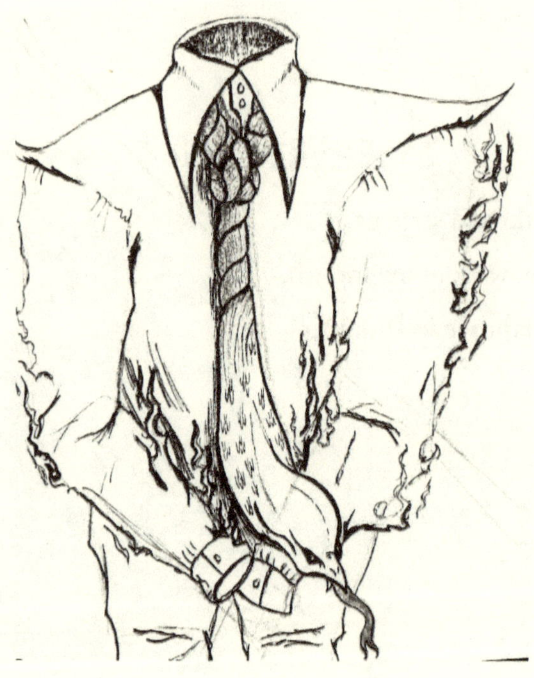

...show mercy to those whose faith is wavering. Rescue others by snatching them from the flames of judgment... but do so with great caution, hating the sins that contaminate their lives.

~ Jude 1:22-23

Preheat

–head in the oven one night.
Not bright. Nothing to admire.
But then, like a knight or esquire to a king–
with a bend at the knee
to kneel and kiss the ring of fire;
'twas a royal thing– it won't working.
"Set to broil?" I think.
But that's too hot;
doing too much
so I give it up.
For another day
I'll give it another shot.
Another shot.
Another shot
of Henny or Hypnot.
Drunkin' stupor
reminds me there's more to the plot.
More to live for.
To step away from death's door;
and close the oven shut.

That is why we never give up... For our present troubles are small and won't last very long. Yet they produce for us a glory that vastly outweighs them and will last forever!
~ 2nd Corinthians 4:16-17

So get rid of all malice. Be done with all deceit, hypocrisy, jealousy, and all unkind speech. ~ 1st Peter 2:1

Be.

Never self-delete.

Troubles are temporary.

Have courage to Be.

Done.

I'm done, sick of it-

queazy. Such a hypocrite.

I've become sleazy.

The heart is deceitful above all things, and desperately wicked: who can know it? ~ Jeremiah 17:9

For everything in the world—the lust of the flesh, the lust of the eyes, and the pride of life—comes not from the Father but from the world. ~ 1st John 2:16

Heart of Deceit

...I've longed to move on from this bane.
Yet nothing works; numb to the pain–
it seems to be plain as day:
that I've no sense of empathy.
I've learned nothing. I mean, really,
what's the point of a Masters
if I'm still enslaved to the inner me?
To the degree that my selfish side,
will oftentimes bite the hand that feeds me.
I've been so greedy,
filled with pride;
an adulterer at heart,
with selfcontrived
notions of who I think I am–
of who I think you see...
I've spun lies so dark,
so as to conceal my deceit–
to deny and depart
from the hurt I bequeathed.
Unfortunately, it continues to grow
like a weed beneath dirt and feet.

And no wonder, for Satan himself masquerades as an angel of light. ~ 2nd Corinthians 11:14

Untitled II

Manipulation,
it comes easy to us all-
do *this* to gain *that*.
We convince and cap.
Put on an act– a façade.
Like catfish– a trap.
Lead others on.
Display phony personas.
But what's the reality?
We're not all that great.
Demand the most from others
yet fall short ourselves.
Judgemental, selfish,
unforgiving, yet in need
of grace; ignorant.

FLAWS

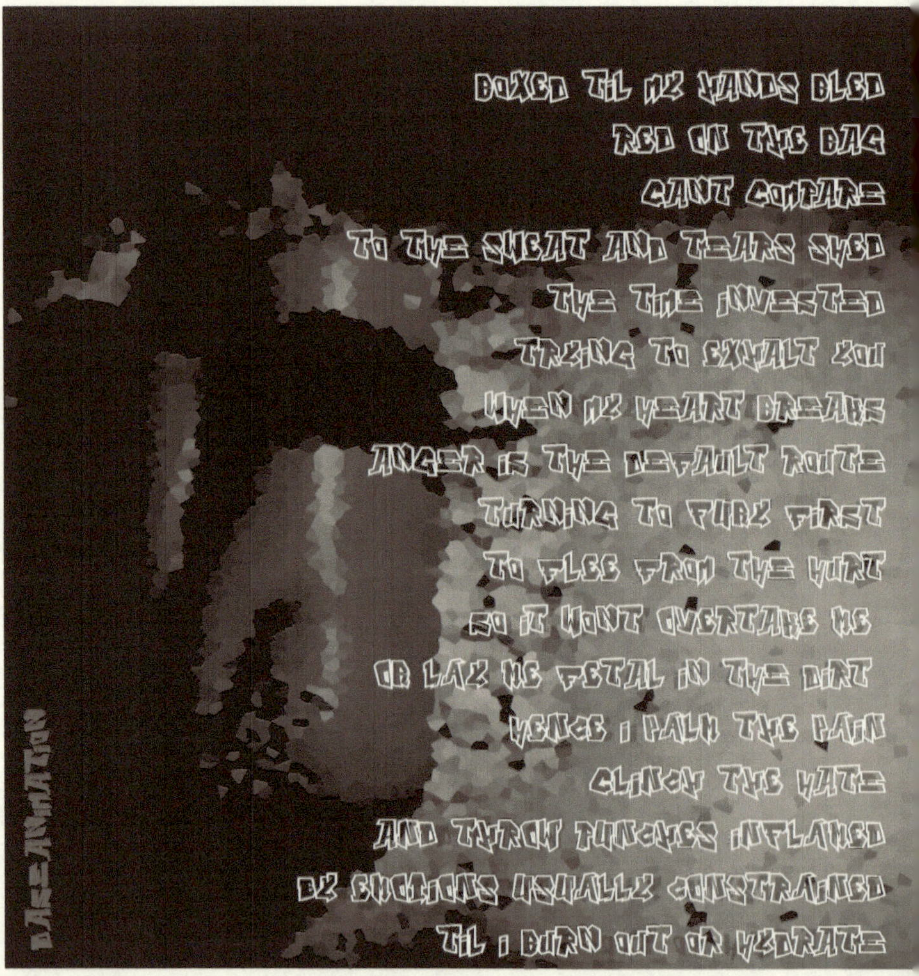
BOXED TIL MY HANDS BLED
RED ON THE BAG
CANT COMPARE
TO THE SWEAT AND TEARS SHED
THE TIME INVESTED
TRYING TO EXHALT YOU
WHEN MY HEART BREAKS
ANGER IS THE DEFAULT ROUTE
TURNING TO FURY FIRST
TO FLEE FROM THE HURT
SO IT WONT OVERTAKE ME
OR LAY ME FETAL IN THE DIRT
HENCE I PALM THE PAIN
CLINCH THE HATE
AND THROW PUNCHES INFLAMED
BY EMOTIONS USUALLY CONSTRAINED
TIL I BURN OUT OR HYDRATE
DASEANIMATION

Fists of Fury

Boxed til my hands bled.
Red on the bag
cant compare
to the sweat and tears shed.
The time invested
trying to exalt You.
When my heart breaks,
anger is the default route.
Turning to fury first
to flee from the hurt,
so it wont overtake me
or leave me fetal in the dirt.
Hence I palm the pain,
clinch the hate,
and throw punches inflamed
by emotions usually constrained
'til I burn out or hydrate.

Let love be without hypocrisy. Abhor what is evil. Cling to what is good. ~ Romans 12:9

For by one offering He has perfected forever those who are being sanctified. ~ Hebrews 10:14

Fraudulent

I wanna love God:
Gotta follow what He taught.
To not be a fraud.

$P \neq P$

I'm trying my best.
Instead of my perfection,
Focus on progress.

I acknowledge my transgressions: and my sin is ever before me.

~ Psalms 51:3

And such were some of you: but you were washed, you were sanctified, you were justified in the name of the Lord Jesus Christ and by the Spirit of our God. ~ 1st Corinthians 6:11

Praise Him Anyway

Lord I love you so much
for helping me out with my crutch.
Couldn't praise you enough
for what you did for me,
showed up when I had a dire need.
Justa dyin' in sin.
Residin' in me
was my sinful self
that ain't wanna repent.
Ain't wanna give in
to you or the Word.
No submission to the gospel I heard.
But this life's a dead end–
this selfish lifestyle
with all my mistakes, failures,
shame and regret.
All the times I knew better
yet couldn't care less.
To me it didn't matter,
who got hurt.
I was wild.

'Til God came and saved me;
Made me His child.
His Grace and mercy,
forever I'll enjoy and grin.
Made me a new creature.
A better boy.
A better friend.
And then a husband,
with a new mind.
Restored my soul,
corrected my heart.
He paid the tole;
My U-turn was just the start.
Now I'm sold,
and will never depart
from the God who cared.
Who, me, He never forgot.

III

FLOWS

Rogue Zulu

Ayo, I'm Rogue Zulu!
I stay rappin' wit' my 2 dudes;
we not a 2-bit rap crew.
That's my squad!
I might cut you
if you cross;
I'm an Xman!
Gloves come off,
Imma mu-tant.
A cool cat,
I mew taunts.
Stand above you
on haunch—
high horse.
Now, of course
I could show you—
better yet, I could tell—
but read on I implore you.
See what's in store,
what's for sale...

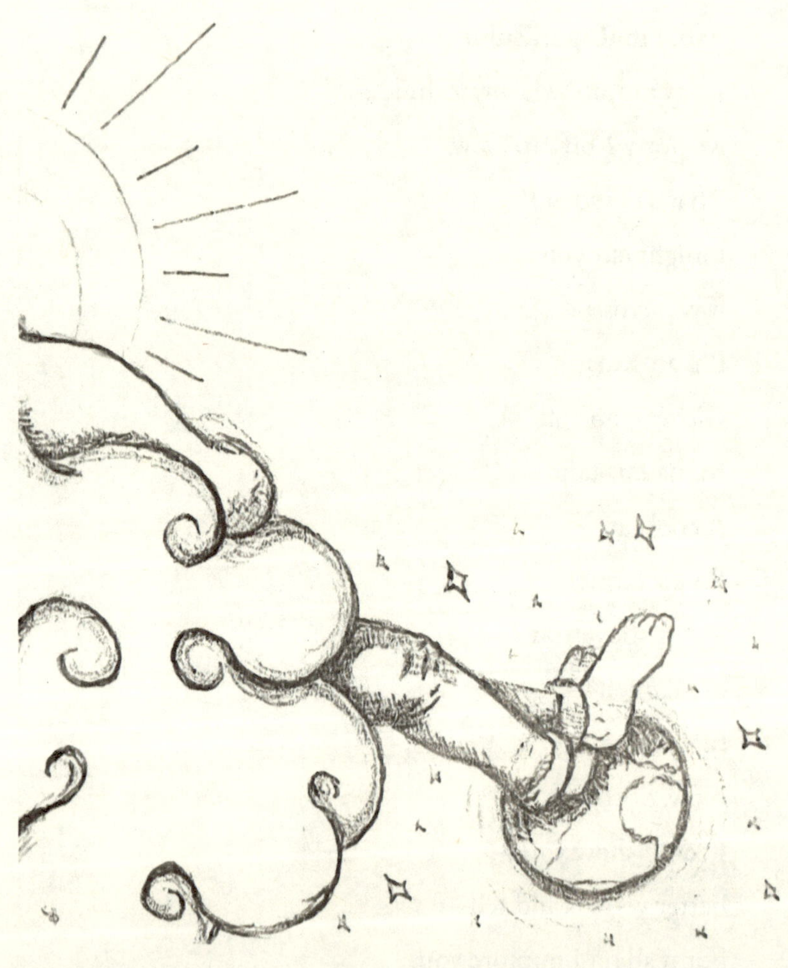

Marvel at this

So just for you imma make it clear, and be Crystal.
Come marvel at His *all power*, it's elemental.
He got that fire, that heat,
put a spark to a tree.
He make that grimy, that real:
from the dust, He revealed us.
And His flow ain't no joke.
Liquid GOAT for ya throat.
Now run it back, those first lines.
Check the easter egg reference:
This a comic book rhyme
bouta inhuman, omnipresent,
Father of time.
Da One above All.
Da Son who still shines.

What do people gain from all their labors at which they toil under the sun? Generations come and generations go, but the earth remains forever ~ Ecclesiastes 1:3-4

Artificial

It bothers me heavily
how the real world we live in
is made artificially .
Our meat with food coloring;
our streets– asphalt covering
good ground and grass.
Beneath this fake societal mask
is our roots and our pasts.
They say life is stranger than fiction
but what's strangest
is we store life savings here–
intention being to appear
as if we have it all together.
But deep down we know
it's done out of fear.
Don't we understand by now
to store our treasure
in the by and by.
Things made by human hands
can't withstand
Fathertime.

Turn to me and have mercy, for I am lonely and in deep distress. ~ Psalms 25:16

Lorn

I enter my internship nervous.

I say "Hi!"

At once, I discern lip service,

they ask "Why, how d'ya do on this day?"

And I reply "I'm fine; really I can't complain."

But it's a lie–

I'm not and I most definitely can.

I overthink my place in this land:

Don't quite understand why

I'm afraid that Imma die soon

if I'm not paid attention to...

I simply try to make it through life.

In dire need of real aid,

I try to sire good deeds,

and overwrite mistakes.

Riddled with anxiety

from this lonely reality;

It leaves my mind on 10.

I'm not fine but I can't overextend.

I want to relax but I'm here instead,

anxious to the max with lorn thoughts in my head.

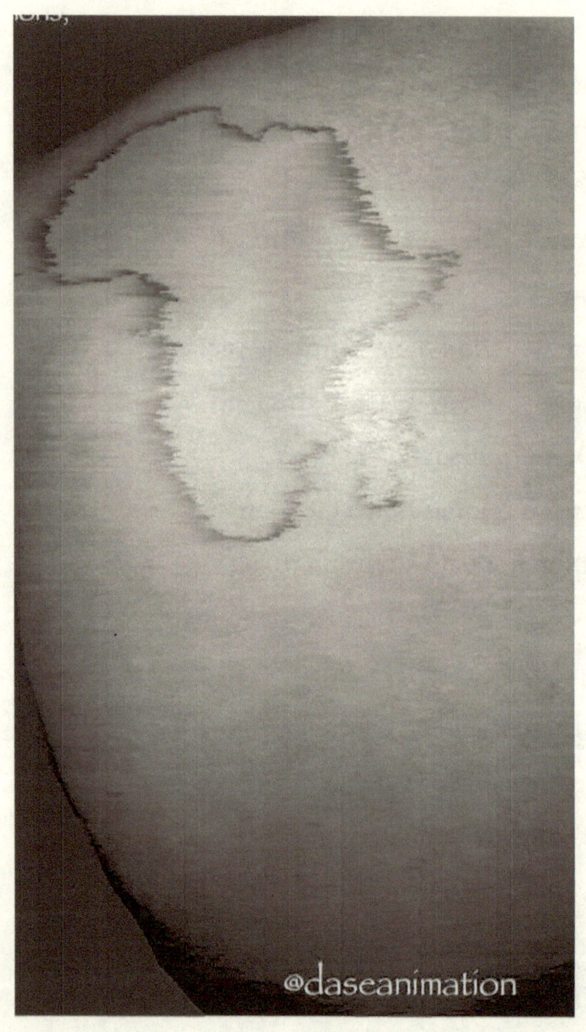
@daseanimation

Africa

Placed on my back,
my place of origins.
You may ask where I'm from,
well I'm Carolinian.
But what I had in mind
was to get a tattoo
with deeper meanin',
to represent roots–
The Motherland.
You see, I'm African– American by force.
For years they endorsed
slave trade– lacked remorse–
and paved, why of course,
the way for circumcision;
the kind that cuts away at traditions
and our memory of before...
And my shoulder blade,
where the tattoo is wore,
stays blank.
Only an outline of the continent;
defining my predicament:
I don't know the truth
of where I really hail.

My brown skin's the only proof
of a slave ship sailed...
Slave migration,
Emancipation,
then Jim Crow and segregation.
Assassinations, cocaine,
incarceration– the sin remains.
Our so-called Nation moves on,
with no reparations.
Free at last but
cut off from our past.
Told to put it behind us,
to move forward.
Can't rewind, thus/therefore
we forget...
So far removed from the truth
I legit, don't know/can't prove,
the part of Africa
they stole our roots...
And 'til I learn more,
the shape of it
will stay a silhouette.
Filled in with Black skin.

Nothing in all creation is hidden from God. Everything is naked and exposed before His eyes... ~ Hebrews 4:13

Supreme

Chicken nuggets.
I'm so real.
Not a fake nugget
like a happy meal.

Gotta eat.
'til I've had my fill.
Make my own money–
Greed... I feed my face.

Lay back in old age,
Wipe my mouth,
and rub my tummy.
Relieved.

I'm a King.
A Boss Nugget.
Supreme.

Karate

I'm clever, witty;
Come through, get dealt wit' swift-
Li, Bruce, Chan-Jackie.

MissileToe

I kick in ya do'
kiss of death– get blown away.
Call that missle-toe.

Erupt

I'm bouta blow up
like mountain Vesuvius!
Volcanic eruption–
yeah man, I'm studious.
I know a lil' bout a lot.
There's mo' to me, a thicker plot.
Da world grows colder,
so strike while it's hot.
Dreads to my shoulders,
long like a mane.
Crown on my head.
Yeah, I'm Lion King.
No pride, just ego.
An August Leo.
Zulu be da name.
Wit' da Rogues, I go.

Go with the...

I might be the most focused man I'll ever know.
Put the work in, at class & the job– to and fro.
I gotta pass & scadaddle bro, hit the road fa' sho.
I gotta hun'ed, then an A; man, I'm on a roll.
Didn't list deans, but aye I'm honor roll.
At day's end, I lay in bed gone.
Dreamin' 'bout a life I been wantin' so long.
When will it be? 4 years, 5?
Maybe the latter
cuz *soon* never arrives.
Take it day by day
Keep my eyes on the prize;
Find a way to grow &

–Go with the flow

Movin'

I'm DaSean C.
I B on my A game.
Animation degree.
Keep it movin', gravy train.
I'll be provin' I ain't a lame.
Makin' money, make it rain
down blessings on those who came
before me & payin' it forward.
The art I do, the only thing I knew.
Drew and drew 'til ECU.
Stretched and grew.
Learned a few things,
remained on the move.
Putting in work,
after class I stay behind.
I'll be fine, sleep when I rip...

Night Flight

Most nights I dream of flying.
Not soaring in the clouds,
but floating over crowds-
those friends and foes of mine,
biding their time in the hall.
I hover to class
and try not to fall.
The tension in the air is palpable,
as high as my altitude.
I rise above teenage attitudes
and give my bullies a scare,
as I barrelroll in midair.
Most nights I dream of flying—
as lucid as can be—
although some nights I don't;
that's fine with me.
The sky will be there,
for me to dive into later.

Let no one look down on your youthfulness, but become an example of the faithful—in speech, in conduct, in love, in faithfulness, and in purity. ~ 1st Timothy 4:12

When I was a child, I talked like a child, I thought like a child, I reasoned like a child. When I became a man, I put away childish things. ~ 1st Corinthians 13:11

Manhood

By Da'Sean Clark

As a child, you're
naive
Just a lil' boy,
bothersome you are
But when Dad's
around
You love, fear and
respect him
Manhood
As a teenager, you're
too cool
Tempers flare and
hormones rage
But you control
yourself
Maturity is setting in
Manhood
As a young man,
you're free
Restrictions are gone
Temptation arouses
But a Man acts his
age
Manhood
As a father, you
have a newfound
responsibility
Family comes first
Everything else
second
You have a son, and
you must teach him
Manhood

Da'Sean Clark, 14, South Central High School.

Father Figures

Had a dream my fathers were friends.
They were cordial and got along;
won't fake for me, or for pretend.
It seemed all wrong,
Although, I treated them equally,
appreciating both,
in reality
one tried his best– at most–
while the other was there for me.
Wild how the ones you resemble,
will leave you be–
-hindsight is always 20/20 though.
Grudges & hate, I never let it go,
for there was none to hold onto in the first place.
But the second the space was filled by another,
felt weird to ever call my new dad Father.
So I didn't; kept it on a solid nickname basis.
With college and dorms, came new faces,
then new knowledge, norms,
awareness of good graces...

I was blessed to have a father,
to grow up toxic free- like a liver.
Provided for, without a worry.
And now I figure,
to be the man I wanna be,
I need to plan to spend more time with family.
To build a stronger bond with my dad,
either or is cool;
at least before
I leave for Grad school.

...your old men shall dream dreams, and your young men shall see visions. ~ Joel 2:28

Surely I am only a brute, not a man; I do not have human understanding. I have not learned wisdom, nor have I attained to the knowledge of the Holy One. ~ Proverbs 30:2-3

Juice

Dreams are worth the squeeze.

Mine are 'specially lucid.

Creative juices.

Untitled III

Drunk beers, sipped knowledge:

Hadn't learned a thing from

four years in college.

You've had enough in the past of the evil things that godless people enjoy– their immorality and lust, their feasting, drunkenness, wild parties, and worship of idols.

~ 1st Peter 4:3

Soul

They got cravings with a K;
would take kanings to the A.
When they'd ring, I'd [p]sigh
–always asking me to pay
for drugs, food, and liquor.
Used to drive me lupe.
I'm glad I ran away–
before they hurt me soul–
evading the sands...

That was the day the hazing grew old,
and my knowledge of the Divine grew Ninefold–
the Spirit pulling me from serving idols.
That's when learning to stroll
and wanting to wear crimson symbols
would fail to compare
to true faith, real fellowship,
and a fully intact
Christ-filled soul.

FLOWS

Reality

Dreamt last night I became a statistic.
Cops beat me
broad daylight wit' da nightstick.
Face on the pavement, knee in my back, it
hurt so much; felt so realistic.
I did nothing wrong,
I was where I should be.
But they aint care–
cops threatened to shoot me.
Was dared to fuss, flinch or tussle.
Couldn't wait to kill
if I moved another muscle.
5.O with the taser
(truth is, looked like a cattle prod);
shocked me in my back,
ruthless but what's kinda odd is
the cops were black.
Imagine that.
See the issue with police brutality.
Is it's about more than race,
it's a mentality...
And this was more than a dream,
It's a reality.

Black Figurines

I'm at my grandma's house;
a usual Mother's Day like it used to be.
Livingroom is packed,
filled with all the family.
Great aunts and uncles laugh amongst themselves.
Great-great grand babies stand wobbly,
steadied by shelves
that're filled with Black Figurines
and glass angel pieces–
polaroid pictures sitting between their creases.
I go outside to get some air.
There, the guys are standing, talking;
they share jokes and info, blow smoke and window-
tinted shades keep them too cool
to go inside... to socialize in the family pool.
I head for the car and suddenly
I see two kids on a bench in front of me.
My cousins laying there,
passed out, got too hot.
Bees and wasps play on their fingers;
I swat them away.
But still they linger.
I swat harder and they begin to swarm,

to form a storm, a hurricane of *hornets;*
tore everything apart.
Grandma's house demolished.
Black figurines fly free,
un-abolished.

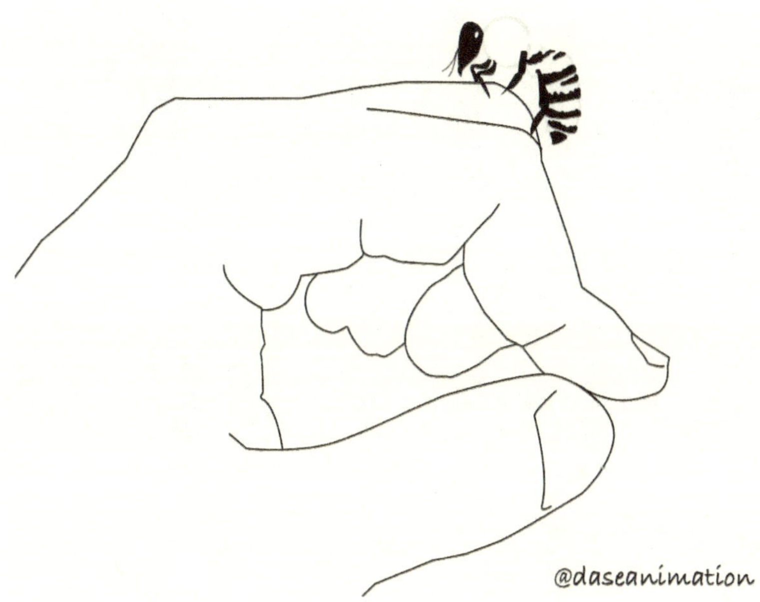

"Jesus, remember me when you come into your kingdom."

~ Luke 23:42

Remembrance

You betta
M, I, crooked letter, crooked letter, M, E
when I'm gone.
Blow up my phone...
Don't leave me 'lone.
Don't lemme be.
You betta weep–
when it's my time,
and I've resigned,
to R.I.P.

Passion+Pain

You would think that art relaxed me...
that music soothed me.
It often does the opposite now.
I thought making my hobby a career would be dope.
Challenging and fun but nope.
My passion's now my pain.
I stress day in and day out;
my thoughts on a night train, lost.
Always focused on the next project,
I lose myself in it but when all is said and done,
I still held something in...
This work didn't casc my lornful thoughts
or douse those fiery feelings.
Self destruction is still inevitable.
This blaze inside must be quenched.
Finally, the other day, I felt it was;
hence I'll try it once again:
With frustration packed into every punch
a Boxing gym left me too sore
to abhor life anymore :)

We know that all things work together for the good of those who love God, those who are called according to His purpose.

~ Romans 8:28

For everyone who asks receives; the one who seeks finds; and to the one who knocks the door will be opened. ~ Matthew 7:8

FOCUS

Ridin' round in my Ford
Focus, Focus,
I must Focus on Him.
He is my Lord, Jesus,
to whom I owe the sum
of my life, my peace,
my wife, this car,
all that I see, and that's taken place so far,
and all that I'll one day start to undergo.
I rejoice for I know
He has so much more in store,
for the good of those who love Him,
who knock knock at his door.
It's a choice to be still at ease, and pray
to hear His gentle voice speak.
Without a doubt, without delay–
good things *will* come
to those who wait.
Trust in Him, have some faith,
watch Him work; be blown away
as you cooperate with His Spirit.
His power & His grace,
transforms all who roam near it.

...two can stand back-to-back and conquer; and a threefold cord is not quickly broken. ~ Ecclesiastes 4:12

23

What does One get
when Two primes combine
into a double digit,
and rhymes with a couple different
words, like Hennesy?
The equivalency of
a bird to a honeybee.
{As in two birds with one stone,
and trihedral ends of a honeycomb}.
Akin to my 2nd degree in Animation,
Followed by the number of years since completion.
It's the popular Psalm
of God's provision.
His peace and calm,
Rod/staff protection.
It's the back-2-back who conquer,
while the braided cord won't unravel.
On your feet when you travel the ball,
and his Bull's jersey– the Greatest of all time.
Tall as Charlie Brown's tree,
(mine is still up, I'll admit)
It's the number *23*.
It's the number of lines writ.

GRATEFULNESS

Yes, I'm grateful for the things
that you have done.
I'm grateful for the things
I've overcome.
On and on and on
You have won;
and on and on my behalf,
You gave Your own Son.
You gave so I could laugh
without fear of the future.
You gave so it would suit your
compassionate nature.
So I'll praise You,
yes I'll bask in,
this Grace everlastin'.
Flowing from my heart
is Gratefulness for traveling
round the world, near and far.
Gratefulness for my girls;
Gratefulness for my wife;
Gratefulness for the two car garage we both like.

Gratefulness for my job–
makin' money is pretty nice.
Gratefulness that the great list
of my mistakes don't exist,
cause You forgave those sins;
clothed me in righteousness.
Gratefulness to taste & see *Your* Goodness.
Gratefulness for my hands–
by You I'm talented.
So understand this:
Flowing from my heart
is Gratefulness for my art.
Gratefulness for rhyme schemin'
and favor from Him.
Gratefulness to finish this
labor of love–
inspired from above–
my book of poems.

AMEN

Thank you for reading.
May these words echo beyond the page...

...He who began a good work in you will carry it on to completion until the day of Christ Jesus.

~ Philippians 1:6

May the LORD bless you & protect you.
May the LORD smile on you & be gracious to you.
May the LORD show you his favor & give you his peace.
~ Numbers 6:24-26

ABOUT THE AUTHOR

DáSean Clark is a Christian, Artist & Animator who uses his creativity as a means to reflect, express, and grow. Much of the writing in this book began simply as journal entries— private prayers, grievances, and moments of honesty that slowly found rhythm and a rhyme scheme on the page. Visual storytelling has long been DáSean's passion and primary medium to work in, while written prose has always been a close second. He loves reading and almost all things grammar (i.e Scrabble, word puzzles, scriptwriting, and rhetorical debates). When he isn't creating, DáSean is rooted in family time with his wife and their two daughters, learning daily what it means to live faithfully and love deeply.

DáSean shares *Faith, Flaws and Flows* with humility and the hope that others may recognize familiar echoes in their own journey.

www.ingramcontent.com/pod-product-compliance
Lightning Source LLC
LaVergne TN
LVHW090520110826
845146LV00003B/927

* 9 7 9 8 2 1 8 9 3 5 0 8 5 *